Fusion

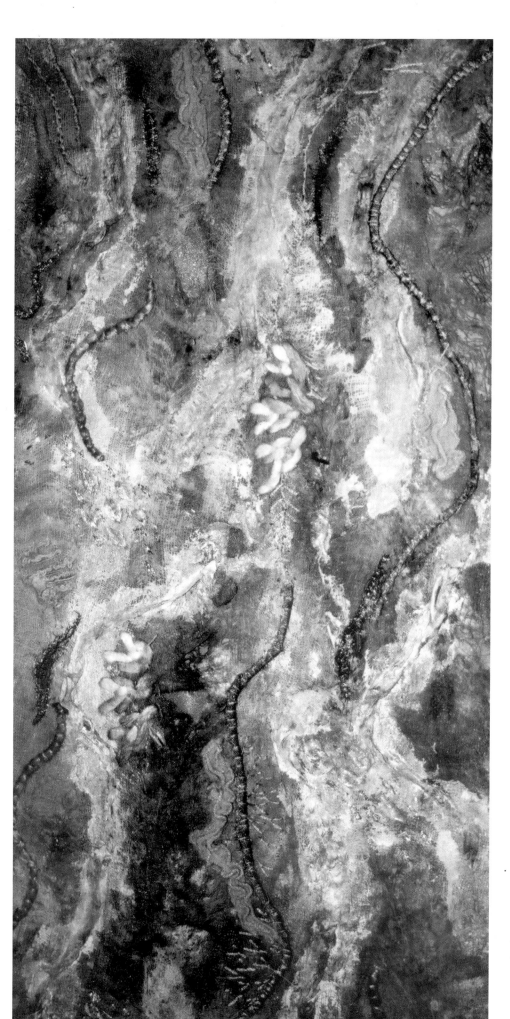

Caroline Amory
Carolyn Browne
Susan Cranwell
Rosalind Dickinson
Bridget Dixon
Sandra Duff
Marian Harrington
Madelaine Nightingale
Gwen Rix
Anne Shearcroft
Phillippa Simons
Norma Tallin
Pauline Verrinder
Pat Watkins

Fibrefusion are all members of
Pauline Verrinder's textile art
workshop group, and meet
fortnightly at Brickworks in
Cambridge.

Beyond Boundaries

INTRODUCTION

Gone are the days when embroidery was solely about stitch and embellishment. Mixed media techniques are a very strong element of the creative embroidery world and this diversity is perhaps the reason why so many of us enjoy the challenge that is textile art.

This book, based on the aims of our workshop is geared towards you and your friends – people who have acquired many of the basic techniques. You enjoy attending day schools and workshops and are striving to find a way forward to develop your own style yet stay motivated. Why don't you draw on your own skills and travel beyond the boundaries?

FOREWORD

I have known the members of the Fibrefusion for some time and have admired their work. This book explores the use of mixed media in textiles in a logical and innovative way. I am sure that it will inspire all the readers to try their own experiments and incorporate the ideas into their own work.

Maggie Grey

We would like to thank:
Maggie Grey
Sandra Duff – Photography
Caroline Hutt – Cartoons
Liz Marley – Proofreading
Hatt/Owen Design – Design
John Theobald – Back and Front Cover Photographs

Suppliers
Art Van Go
1 Stevenage Road, Knebworth, Herts SG3 6AN
01438 814946

Inca Studio
10 Duke Street, Princes Risborough, Bucks HP27 0AT
01844 343343

Acrylic Wax, Angelina Fibres, Bondaweb, Brusho, Irisé Film, Kunin, Vilene and Xpandaprint are registered trade names.

To order the book telephone 01728 860190 or 01954 260358

CONTENTS

Top: An exercise in layers including paper beads/sticks and wire

Centre: Layers with machine stitching

Right: Wrapped wire frame with stitched fabric insertions

1 Fusion of fabric, fibre and stitch

MENU
- Fabric
- Layering
- Fusing and Bonding
- Stitch

Throw away your inhibitions! As creative people, we relish the opportunity to experiment with all that is new, whilst still preserving the talents and skills we have gained over the years. Our cupboards and drawers are bursting at the seams with fabrics, threads and those untried new products. Let's begin with these.

Fabrics

Fabric is the predominant material used by a creative embroiderer, and along with threads is certainly one of our many vices. The following list is just a memory jogger for the execution of that perfect technique for your project.

MANIPULATION	Pleat, tuck, fold, crease, manipulate	Gather, knot, plait, weave, drape	Roll, twist, coil, pinch
APPLIQUE	Appliqué by stitch (hand and machine), bond, glue, fuse	Apply fabric, paper, metal, plastics, wire, mesh, felt	Turned edges, frayed, satin stitch, couched, singed, burnt
REVERSE APPLIQUE (Cutting back)	Several layers of lightweight fabrics	Mix different types of fabric	Sheers on top, silk & felt below
PATCHING AND PIECING	Conventional patchwork techniques	Rough edges, distort, unusual fabrics, paper, hand dyed fabric	Surface decoration, paint, machine & hand stitch, bonding, beads & found objects, embellishment
QUILTING	Hand & machine techniques	Unconventional threads, strips of fabric	Pin, staple, tie
LAYERS	Stitched by hand or machine, slashing & sculpting through layers	Bonded, fused with soldering iron	Mixed media e.g. fabric, paper, metals, wire mesh, plastics, felt
PAINTS AND DYES, AND OTHER SURFACE COLOURING MEDIA	Printing, painting, stencilling, discharge, screen printing, silk painting, batik	Embossing, transfer paints	Fibre reactive dyes, acid dyes, natural dyes, silk dyes
CUTTING AND SLASHING	Slash and sculpt through layers	Cut back through layers of different fabrics	Cutting and slashing with soldering iron
EMBELLISHMENT	Stitch (hand & machine), beads, cords, ribbons, braids, paints	Wire, metals, found objects	Plastics, paper, felt

Opposite: Layers of lace and sheers bonded. Couched cords and woven wheels

Layers

Some of the most interesting and tactile surfaces for stitch are made up of layers of fabric. The types of fabric used can be varied, with multiple layers of a lightweight fabric creating a malleable material useful as a base for many surface decoration techniques. The methods for sandwiching the fabrics together can vary from, bonding, fusing with a soldering iron, to using low tack glue or simply tacking layers together as a precursor to further embellishment.

Layering Experiment One – Place eight or ten layers of fine fabric (muslin works well) one on top of another and tack firmly together. As an option, try using different coloured layers or different types of fabric. Mark your design on the top layer. Work reverse appliqué by outlining the design with two rows of machining. Cut back through the layers of fabric with a sharp pair of scissors or a soldering iron, using your design as a guide, to reveal the chosen colours below.

Layering Experiment Two – Work the above technique with eight to ten layers using lightweight natural fibre fabrics, suitable for dyeing with fibre reactive dyes or silk paints diluted with 25% water. As before, machine around the design twice. When cutting back, only cut through half the layers to leave a thicker base of fabric on the underside. Make up your dyes for the direct dyeing method. After stitching, dampen the resulting fabric with water. Ensure that the moisture has absorbed into all the fibres. Using your design as a guide, paint or sponge the made-up dyes directly onto the stitched fabric. Inevitably the colours will bleed on contact, this effect increases the richness of the technique. Embellish with hand or machine stitch.

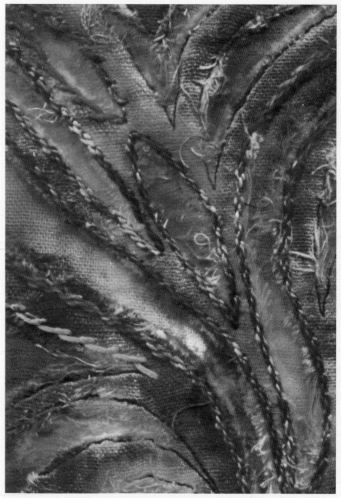

Above right: Layering experiment two

Below: Layers of textured fabric sheers and paint, machine and hand stitched, distressed with hot air tool

Why don't you try...

All the following suggested layering techniques are only a starting point. Try other layers of materials and media to enable you to achieve that perfect tactile fabric for your design. Read the following list from left to right and use it as an optional list of combinations for layers, mixing and matching if wished. All will need embellishment to secure.

Always use a respirator mask when using heat with plastics and synthetic materials. Work in a well ventilated room.

		BOTTOM LAYER	MIDDLE LAYER	TOP LAYER
FUSING	Sandwich these layers of material between two pieces of baking parchment using *Bondaweb* as the bonding agent.	• Plastics	Chopped fabrics, threads, paint	Plastics
		• Plastic or cellophane	Chopped fabrics, threads, sequins, leaves, petals	Bonded chiffon
		• *Angelina* fibre	Threads, chopped fabrics	*Angelina* fibre
		• Calico, muslin, cotton	Threads	Carded cocoon strippings
		• Carded cocoon strippings	Threads, strips of fabric, fabric	Carded cocoon strippings
		• Synthetic felt	Synthetic sheer fabric	Use soldering iron to draw a design and fuse in one
BONDING	Sandwich these layers of material between two pieces of baking parchment before ironing to bond. Not happy with your bonded sandwich? – try bonding a fourth fabric on top, and if necessary a fifth. Try printing, Use the heat gun or soldering iron.	• Craft *Vilene*, felt, fabrics	Threads, chopped fabrics, wilted flower petals	Bonded sheer fabric
		• Fabrics, felt, *Vilene*, velvet	Threads	Bonded *Irisé* film
		• Fabric, felt, *Vilene*, velvet	*Irisé* film	Bonded chiffon
		• Chiffon scarf	Chopped threads, ribbons, fabrics, free machined lace	Chiffon scarf
		• Felt/craft *Vilene*	*Bondaweb*	Chiffon scarf – melted back with heat gun
		• Fabric, felt, craft *Vilene*	Bonded snips of lace	Bonded net, bonded melted chiffon
		• Choice of fabric	Bonded lengths of a mixture of threads scattered evenly	Bonded old lace shawl or lace fabric
		• Plastic sandwich as above	Bonded cut squares/ triangles etc. of fabric, e.g. silk	Chiffon or net
		• Muslin	Bonded handmade or decorated paper	Lightweight cotton scrim
STITCH	Create the sandwich by tacking the layers of fabric firmly together.	• Fabric, *Vilene*, felt etc.	Knitted, crocheted or woven wire (use large needles)	Sheer fabrics or watersolublelace
		• Coloured tights stretched in an embroidery hoop	Chopped fabrics and threads sprinkled onto tights	Sheer fabric pinned firmly near to edge of frame to contain fabric bits. Machine stitch with bold circular movements.
		• Base fabric, wadding, and fabric	Chiffon scarf – melted with heat gun	Net
		• Fabric	Threads	Coloured cold-melt glue gun, piped onto baking parchment, lifted when cold and appliqued

Coloured layers of nappy liners and fabric machined stitched. Heat gun zapped

Layers of fabric and fibres couched threads and cords

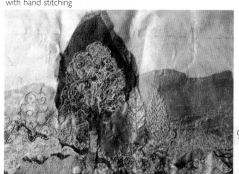

Appliqued fabric embellished with hand stitching

Fusion Layers' Challenge

Create a layered fabric which has multiple uses as a background for surface embellishment.

Work to a colourscheme – any of the fabrics can be hand dyed.

"Of course it's worth it – It took me nearly a year!"

- Make a layered sandwich starting with a cotton fabric, 2oz wadding, silk, sheet of *Bondaweb*, scraps of lace and threads, another layer of *Bondaweb* and a chiffon fabric that melts easily on top. Tack the first three layers together, then bond other layers on top.
- Free machine quite densely all over to create a textural effect and to join all layers together.
- Use a heat gun to melt the patches of unworked chiffon and to reveal areas of lace, threads and silk.
- Lightly scrape *Xpandaprint* or similar medium over the fabric, and expand with the heat gun.
- Carefully work metallic paint lightly over *Xpandaprint*, and to pick up the texture of the lace, threads, and free machining. The surface can be further embellished with free machining or hand stitch.
- Use this fabric as a base to create anything from bags to boxes, book covers or cushions, or use it as a base for a hanging or panel.

Top right: Box based on fossils at Lulworth Cove

Right: Techniques as above

Opposite: More layers

Stitch

Many of us when working through ideas for our next project fall back on those familiar stitches that we can work with confidence, instead of extending our perceived knowledge of traditional stitch.

Why don't you try...

First look at the thread you are using. You can drastically alter a traditional stitch by using an unconventional thread. If the thread is too thick, couch it down. Try mixing the threads in the needle, or any of the ideas below.

"yes, it took me a whole week"

- Thick thread instead of thin
- Thin thread instead of thick
- Thin ribbon
- Thin twisted strips of fabric
- Paper thread
- Fine string – (colour it)
- A thread extracted from a woven fabric, especially if it is crinkled
- Wool, including knobbly yarns
- Knitting cottons
- Fine wire
- Fibres (vegetable, silk, wool, or synthetic)
- Manufactured cords
- Free-machined cords
- Raffia
- Fine sinewy fibres from boiled plant material
- Paper strips
- Thin strips of plastic
- Fishing line

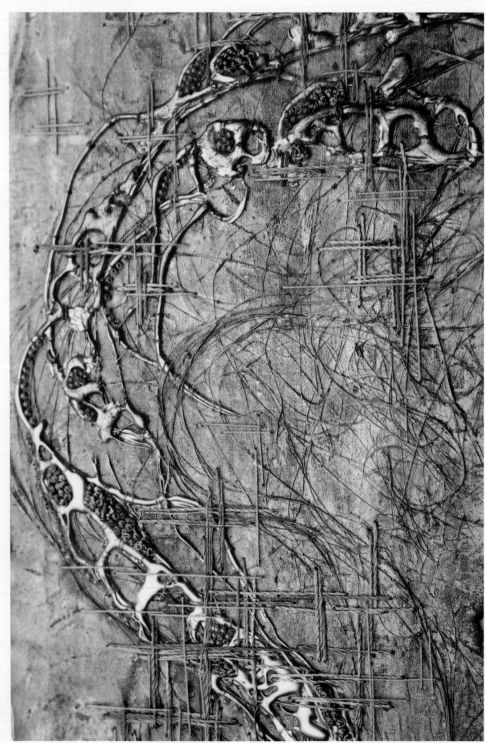

Right: Calico with gesso and linen fibres.
Low melt glue couched on top – embellished
with beads and stitch

Stitch Experiments

- Experiment with linear, composite and isolated stitches. Can you work the stitches in isolation, vary the length, double them up, work them on top of each other or closely side by side?
- Can the stitches be worked over sticks, thicker threads, string or wire or over cords (manufactured or hand-made) or worked slips?
- For traditional stitches the tension has to be even – try varying the tension. Pull it tight, loosen it or a combination of both. Take the basic shape of a stitch, can you stretch it either vertically or horizontally? Can it be twisted or distorted or the traditional shape changed?
- Look at the spacing between stitches – can that spacing be varied either horizontally or vertically?
- Look at the back of the work. How many times do we turn a piece of work over, and decide that we like the back more than the front – exploit this?
- It dosen't matter whether the stitches are perfect or not, just as long as they contribute to the interpretation of your design.

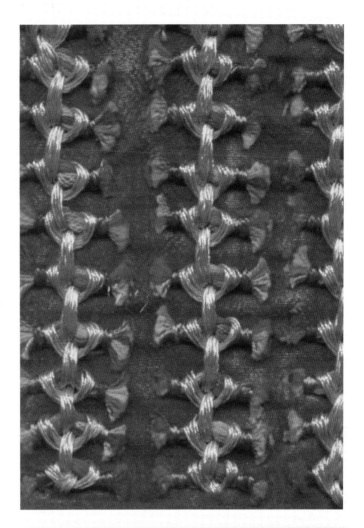

Top right: Raised chain band worked over bars of wrapped, tufted threads

Right: Handstitch over shredded muslin and sticks

2 Paper

MENU
- Tissue Paper
- Abaca Tissue
- Handmade and Decorated Paper

Paper is now an established part of the creative embroiderer's armoury. The inevitable challenge is how to harness the texture, translucency or transparency of the paper. Most papers which can be purchased from art and craft shops can be stitched upon – any type of paper including your own decorated papers are worth a try.

Thought has to be given to the ultimate use and destination of a finished project containing paper. Is the work functional? Can it be cleaned? Will it be placed in a draughty area, possibly resulting in a torn piece of work?

Excessive perforation of the paper with stitch, particularly machine embroidery, can be arrested by bonding a stabilising fabric e.g. muslin to the reverse side. Use this technique also to strengthen a fragile paper, such as tissue.

Layers of 'snow flakes' hand and machine stitched

Paper experiments

Construct a layered textural fabric using tissue paper. In this instance, the tissue is craft tissue, bought from an art or stationery shop. Tissue paper creates a tactile textured surface when glued or bonded to a support.

You will need:
• Tissue (white)
• Calico, cotton or similar plain weave fabric
• PVA glue (diluted with equal amount of water)
• Any colouring medium e.g. *Brusho*, ink, dyes, silk paints etc.
• Wax crayons or acrylic paints or metallic wax

Add colour to your PVA solution and paint fabric completely. Scrunch tissue, then smooth it out carefully. Apply onto the painted fabric, easing out the bubbles. Do not worry if tissue tears – it adds to the textural effect. Re-paint with the same coloured PVA solution. Leave to dry thoroughly. Pick up the high points of the tactile surface by colouring with wax crayons, metallic wax, or a lightly loaded paint brush.

Top right and right: Refers to 'Paper Experiments'

Why don't you try...

Trap any of the following materials between the fabric and tissue:

• Fabric snippets
• Threads
• Pressed flowers
• Leaves
• String
• Decorated papers
• Chopped discarded pieces of embroidery

Try any of the following materials as a base:

• Craft *Vilene*
• Felt including *Kunin* felt
• Decorative paper
• Handmade paper

Use coloured tissue paper instead of using a colouring medium

Above: Hazel twigs and paper

Below and right: Muslin and mulberry paper shaped over mould – hand stitched

Paper experiments

The success of the next experiment relies on the strength of *Abaca Tissue*. Other similar papers are also suitable, i.e. Mulberry Paper, Lens Tissue, Repair Tissue, and others. *Abaca Tissue* retains its strength, even when wet so can be painted, printed, embossed, foiled and manipulated successfully. The tissue can be bonded onto paper, card, fabric or itself. When coated with either linseed oil, diluted PVA or acrylic wax the paper becomes more transparent. Two or more sheets placed together are strong enough to be stitched into by either hand or machine.

This technique uses *Abaca Tissue*, to create a papier mache suitable to stitch upon. You will need:

• *Abaca Tissue*
• Wallpaper paste (diluted with equal amounts of water)
• Muslin or scrim
• A mould e.g. mask, bowl, vessel

Grease your mould lightly with petroleum jelly. Tear *Abaca Tissue* into approximately 2" (5cm) sized pieces. Paste the pieces of torn tissue with wallpaper paste, and place on the mould. Carefully cover the mould with three layers of pasted paper. Cut or tear muslin into small pieces and paste. Completely cover *Abaca Tissue* with muslin pieces. Repeat the above procedure once more, finishing with a layer of muslin.

When the tissue and muslin layers are dry, it is ready for embellishment.

Above right: Abaca tissue shaped over a mould
Below: Bowl using these techniques

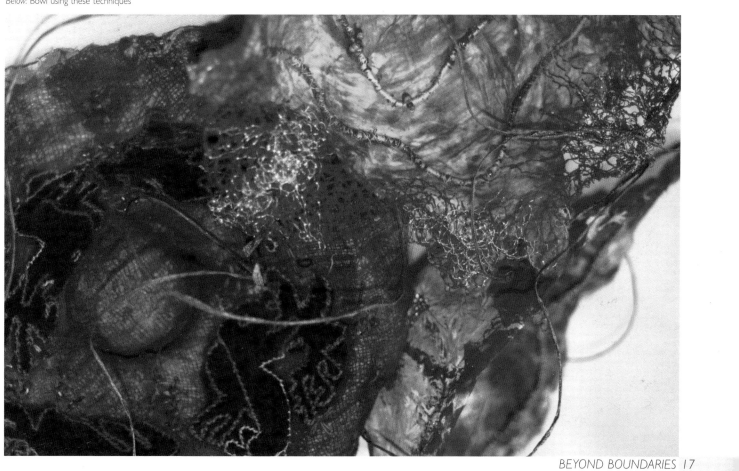

Why don't you try...

- To cover the reverse side of your item, paste another layer of Abaca Tissue and muslin or scrim over the stitching. Several more layers on the reverse side will also strengthen the structure. This layer can be painted, printed or foiled etc.
- Embellish the reverse side of the structure by stitching on framed pieces of muslin or scrim. Then lightly paste and apply these onto the reverse side of the structure.
- Try trapping materials in between the top layers e.g. string or threads, dried flowers or leaves, fabric snippets etc.
- An interesting variation is to wire a 3-D structure made of barbecue sticks, then layer tissue and muslin, both inside and outside. Stitch on muslin and apply as suggested above.
- The tissue and muslin can also be layered on a plastic covered surface to create a fabric to embellish.
- Use this method to create items such as masks, bowls, dishes, plates, vessels, jewellery, hats (for fun only), book covers and lamp shades.

Handmade and decorated paper

Making paper has been a skill that embroiderers have enjoyed for many years. Who doesn't get excited when we see the wonderful ethnic handmade papers in the shops. Decorating our own papers for designwork and stitch has also been an important part of our vocabulary. We have used these papers for making books and boxes, mounted numerous embroidery samples, used them as backgrounds for panels, covering books and wrapping presents – but what about embroidery?

Opposite top: 'Pod vessel'
Opposite: 'Foxy mask'
Below: 'Hydrangea' using handmade papers

Why don't you try...

• If you want to stitch on handmade paper, bond or glue a fabric stabiliser on the reverse side.

• Many of the ethnic handmade papers have fibres incorporated, giving them strength, so light stitching is possible.

• Ethnic handmade paper and thin decorated paper are ideal for manipulation.

• Cut-out or torn shapes can be applied down onto a fabric background.

• Papers used as part of the layering techniques.

• Bond or stitch, torn, distressed, and printed paper down onto a background.

• Stabilise handmade paper, stitch, colour and stiffen with button polish.

Fusion Paper Challenge

Create a richly textured paper-based fabric for embellishment. Don't use the listed ingredients as a recipe, be adventurous and try different materials.

• Bond scrim to the underside of handmade or decorated paper. Leaving a 1cm excess of scrim round all edges of paper is an option. Capitalise on the deckled edge of the handmade paper or tear a decorated paper, re-colouring torn edges and scrim.
• If your choice is handmade paper, colour with acrylics, and lightly embellish with metallic wax taking the colour onto the scrim if used.
• Frame a sandwich consisting of chiffon scarf, shredded pieces of coloured scrim and chiffon scarf. Embellish with stitch, by hand and machine, to create a random ground covering effect.
• Distress chiffon sandwich by using a heat gun.
• Apply distressed stitched pieces to paper background integrating with stitch.
• Use this paper-based textile as a background for your main design.

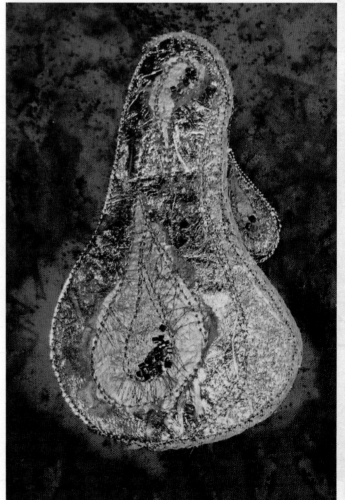

Above right: layers of handmade paper, felt and scrim – hand stitched

Right: Layered experiment using Irisé film

Far right: decorated handmade paper bonded and layered – stitched with a computer pattern on the machine

3 Metallic materials

3 Metallic materials

MENU
• Metals
• Wire
• Paints & foils

Many of us are drawn to the reflective lustre of metallics, often being tempted to enhance our work through their use. With metallics, subtlety is the secret of success. To prevent an overbearing domination of the work by the use of metals, ensure a thorough integration by knocking back the shine with either paints, patina sheers or stitch.

Background – Painted Bondaweb on velvet
Foreground – Handmade decorated papres, muslin, shim
Hand and machine stitched

Metals

METAL MATERIALS	COLOUR & DECORATE	APPLY
Metal shim (aluminium, copper, and brass) from 0.002"	• French enamel varnish • Glass paints • Heat over a flame to colour • Car spray paints • Spirit-based metallic paint • Dark coloured acrylics	Bond Glue Stitch
Drink cans	**To age and distress metals** • Apply household cleaner to brass or copper. • Apply diluted bleach or vinegar	
Brass & copper wire mesh		
Tomato or garlic tubes	• Car spray paints • French enamel varnish • Glass paints • Spirit based metallic paint • Dark coloured acrylics	Bond Glue Stitch

Why don't you try...

When using chemicals, always use a respirator mask, protect your eyes, wear gloves and work in a well ventilated room.

Temporarily attach metal shim to fabric ready for stitching, with low tack spray glue. Machine stitch the metals to a thick fabric, such as felt, coloured and bonded craft *Vilene*, velvet or any firmly woven fabric. Decoration to the metal can take the form of embossing with an old biro, embossing tool, or stitching. Knock the colour back with any of the ideas listed below, stitching, or overlaying with sheers.

Above and right: Machine stitch experiment on copper shim, which has been heated and patinized

Wire

As another medium for use in embroidery, wire has many applications. Initially, as a securing medium in construction, decoratively, or as a structural and firm edging for shapes. It can be trapped between layers of fabric or stitch to create a firm material for manipulation. The wires used can vary from florists' wire, paper covered florists' or cake decorators' wire (can be coloured), crinkled fine gauge wire, and beading wire. Wire can also be extracted from reels of cable.

Knitting, crochet, & weaving – Ideally use 30 gauge or finer, many colours are available. Use wire as a base for embellishment, to apply or to trap between layers of fabric as an aid to firm manipulation of a stitched fabric.

Manipulate and couch – wire can be formed into decorative shapes and couched down onto a fabric base.

Coiling – Use a fine crochet hook or large tapestry needle to coil wire round for the construction of beads or wired coils. There is an inexpensive wire coiling machine on the market for instant results.

Wired edges – when a fine wired edge is required to give a manipulated shape, couch down firmly by hand or zig-zag over the wire by machine and trim back.

Right: Wire as frame and used decoratively

Below: Wire as a framework

Wire experiments

The following technique can be used to create a wired lace fabric which can be used for 3-D items such as vessels, bowls, boxes etc.

- Decide on the item you wish to make and colour a piece of craft *Vilene* to the relevant size.
- Draw a simple design on the craft *Vilene*, either in a symmetrical pattern or randomly.
- Couch the wire down with your machine using a needle size 100, to help prevent needle breakages.
- Using 24 gauge wire, start by laying the end of the wire down for 1cm (¹/₂"), zig-zag over the wire to hold then bend the wire back on itself. See diagram. Satin-stitch carefully from the bend onwards ensuring that the width of the stitch generously covers the wire.
- Follow the line of the design and satin-stitch over the wire until all the lines are covered. Try to use one length of wire for the whole design, doubling the wire where necessary to have one continuous length. This avoids weak spots. Finish as you started by bending the wire and repeat machining. Take care to work slowly and carefully to avoid bending and therefore weakening the wire.
- Once the wire is applied, select only one of the wired areas and cut out the coloured *Vilene*, leaving a few mm. of *Vilene* on the inner edge to be able to anchor your stitching.
- Set your machine for free-machine embroidery and using running stitch, place the needle into the inner edge of the *Vilene*. Machine evenly across the open space until you reach the other side. Repeat this process several times to create an area of lace. This process can be worked to create a patterned lace.
- Repeat the procedure of cutting the *Vilene*, and stitching lace over the whole piece, ensuring that only one area is cut out at a time.
- Tidy up the inner edge of each wired space with satin stitch, working over the edge of the *Vilene*, being careful not to catch the wire.
- Finally, cut away the *Vilene* on the outside of the design, and tidy up the outer edge with satin stitch as before.

" So that's where my gardening glove went!"

Vessel using 'wire experiment' methods

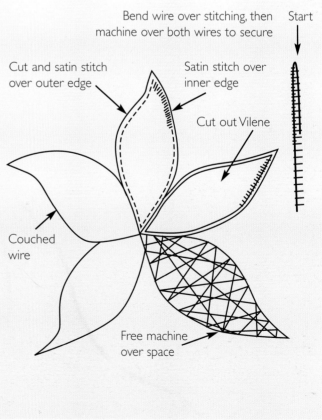

Bend wire over stitching, then machine over both wires to secure   Start

Cut and satin stitch over outer edge

Satin stitch over inner edge

Cut out Vilene

Couched wire

Free machine over space

Metallic paints and foils

METALLIC PAINTS AND COLOURING MEDIA	TECHNIQUES AND USES
Floristry spray paint (non toxic when dry)	• Can be used on any surface including fabric.
Metallic powders **(Always wear a mask when using these powders)**	• To give a clear lustre it is best to use a fabric binder. P.V.A. glue can be used, but it tends to dull the shine. • Try adding to acrylic paints and wax. Try using Acrylic Wax as a binder.
Acrylic paints (metallic colours)	• More flexible than fabric paints as there is no need to heat set. • Can be used successfully on most fabrics. Ideal for printing, painting, stencilling etc on fabric.
Spirit based metallic paint	• Can be used on most surfaces. Very effective floated on water for marbling on fabric and paper.
Metallic embossing powders	• Sprinkle onto an acrylic paint base, then raise with a heat gun. • Wonderful textural effects.
Metallic wax	• Can be applied to a variety of surfaces including fabric. • Can be buffed to a high lustre. Good for accentuating texture.
Transfer paints (no metallic colours, but can be ironed onto metallic surfaces to change colour).	• Iron onto fused *Angelina* Fibres, to increase colour. • Iron onto a card wrapped evenly with metallic. threads to enhance the colour. • Iron onto metal shim. • Iron onto metal foil.

Metallic foils

• Lustrous metallic foils add that extra vitality to a design using metallics which can be transferred onto fabric, paper, plaster, card, wood and many other surfaces
• The foils come in many colours, and are a 'poor mans' version of gold leaf.
• Foils can be transferred by using various glues including P.V.A. glue, or *Bondaweb*.
• The luster can be knocked back by using transfer paints, or by applying acrylics lightly or *Acrylic Wax*.

Right: Scrim, paper and metallic paints
Below: Layered experiment using shim, foils and metallic paints

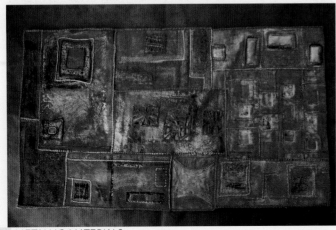

Fusion wire challenge

Create 3-D structures with the aid of wire, by using wired machine cords.

- With this method you can create coiled pots or vessels. Having decided on your project, machine a vast length of cord using fine wire as the core. You can also use machined cords without the wire. Using the traditional coiling method (the same method that we used for making raffia mats as children) and starting from the base, work the cords to create your pot.
- Wired machined cords can be stitched together to create a fabric which can be manipulated into any structural shape.
- Couch wire down by machine, randomly or in patterns all over a fabric base to create a wired material that can be manipulated into any shape or form.

Right: Coiled wire pots

Below: Machine covered wire couched on to fabric

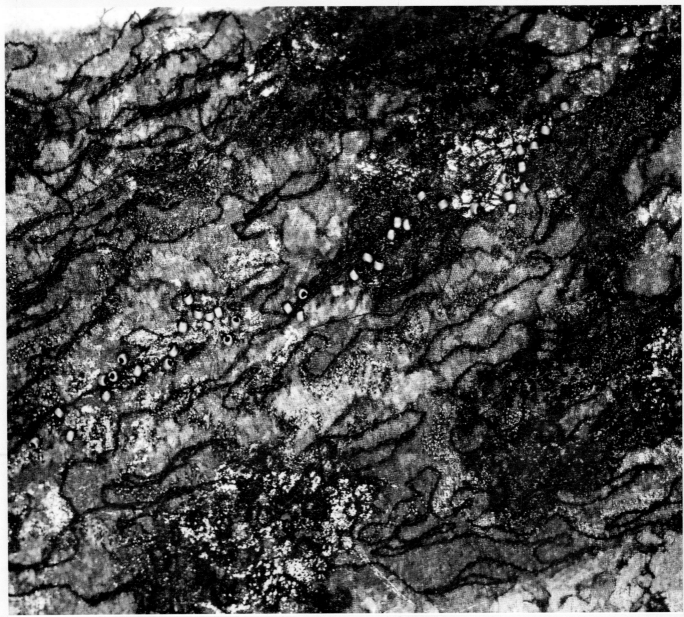

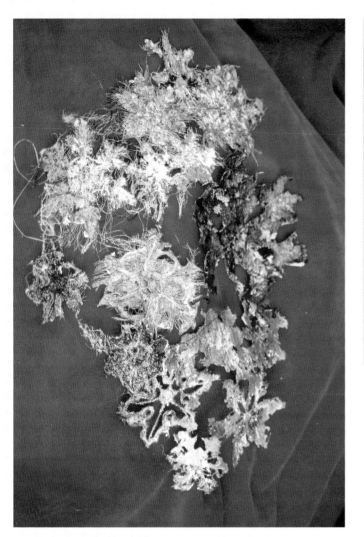

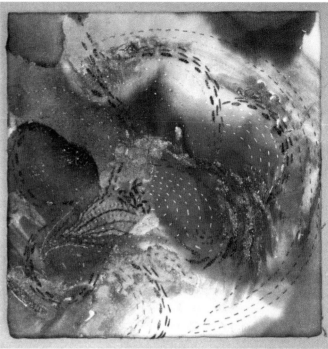

Some examples of techniques covered throughout the book

Pauline, without your inspirational guidance,
none of this would have been possible.
Thank you from all of us.